500004584177

GW01376825

METROPOLITAN BOROUGH OF WIRRAL

Please return this book to the Library from which it was borrowed on or before the last date stamped. If not in demand books may be renewed by letter, telephone or in person. Fines will be charged on overdue books at the rate currently determined by the Borough Council.

012819

018246

016179   015490

391.44

TURNER, D.

Accessories

DEPARTMENT OF LEISURE SERVICES + TOURISM
LIBRARIES AND ARTS

SCHOOLS

ACCESSORIES

Dorothy Turner

Wayland

Costumes and Clothes

Accessories
Children's Clothes
Clothes in Cold Weather
Clothes in Hot Weather
Fashionable Clothes
Hair and Make-Up
How Clothes Are Made
Sports Clothes
Theatrical Costume
Traditional Costume
Uniforms
Working Clothes

Some words in this book are printed in **bold**. Their meanings are explained in the glossary on page 30.

First published in 1989 by Wayland (Publishers) Ltd.
61 Western Road, Hove, East Sussex BN3 1JD.

Cover: Young girls in India wearing beautiful, ornate jewellery as decoration.

Editor: Deborah Elliott
Designer: Ross George

© Copyright 1989 Wayland (Publishers) Ltd.

British Library Cataloguing in Publication Data

Turner, Dorothy, 1944–
    Accessories
1. Fashion. Accessories
I. Title   II Series
391'.44
ISBN 1-85210-381-7

Phototypeset by Kalligraphics, Horley, England
Printed in Italy by G. Canale & C.S.p.A., Turin
Bound in France by A.G.M.

Contents

Chapter 1 — **What are Accessories?**
    The things we wear — 4

Chapter 2 — **Accessories for Fashion**
    All dressed up — 6
    Look at me! — 8
    What accessories can do — 10

Chapter 3 — **Useful Accessories**
    Footwear — 14
    Gloves and scarves — 16
    Hats — 18
    Bags and belts — 20
    Umbrellas — 22

Chapter 4 — **Decorative Accessories**
    Precious jewels — 24
    Jewellery around the world — 26

Chapter 5 — **Accessories from the Past**
    The things they wore! — 28

Glossary — 30
Books to read — 30
Index — 31

Chapter 1

What are Accessories?

The things we wear

Accessories are the many different smaller items of clothing and decoration that we wear – shoes, hats and belts, for example. They are also the things we carry about with us, such as bags and umbrellas, as well as the jewellery we use for personal decoration.

Basic clothing, such as coats, trousers, skirts and jumpers, is needed to protect us

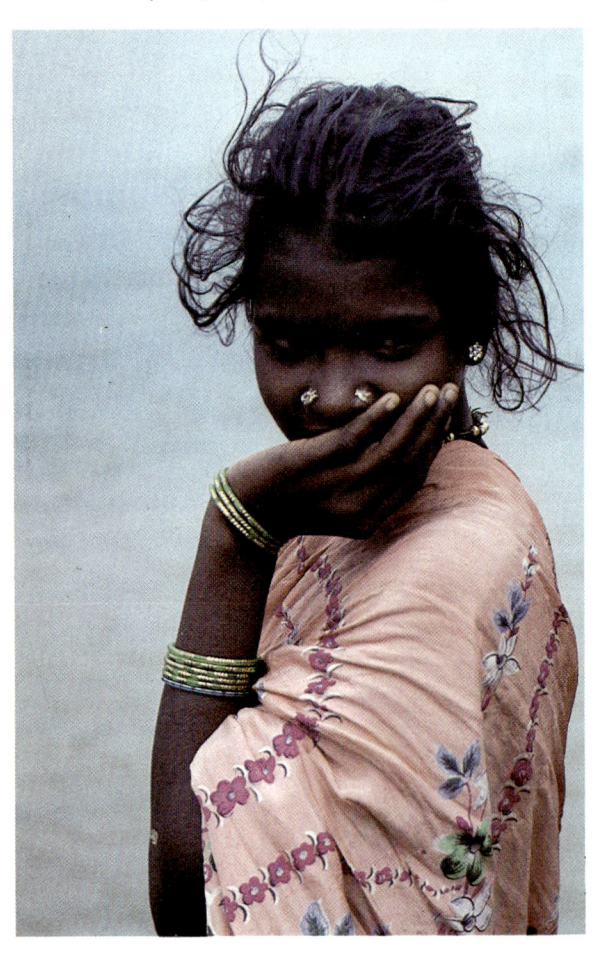

Above **When choosing glasses make sure you select a pair that suit the shape of your face and your hair-style.**

Left **All over the world, people like to decorate their bodies with different types of jewellery.**

from the weather – hot or cold, wet or dry. Accessories are not neccessarily important in this way. Sometimes they are worn for no other purpose than simply for fun. However, most accessories actually do have some function. Shoes, for example, protect our feet from hard ground and sharp stones, although many

Above **Hats, shoes and boots are practical accessories that come in a variety of bright and interesting colours and designs.**

Right **There are lots of unusual and fashionable sun-glasses available that can liven up summer outfits.**

people manage without any shoes at all in warmer climates. Gloves, bags and hats also serve a useful purpose – gloves and hats keep our hands and heads warm and bags are useful for keeping things in.

Many of the things we wear as accessories are worn just because we enjoy dressing up. In theory, there could be just one style of clothing for everyone to wear – but that would be very boring and dull. So we liven our clothes up with ribbons, badges, bows and buttons. The accessories we wear can be one of the most important ways we have of telling people who we are and what we are like.

Chapter 2

Accessories for Fashion

All dressed up

Accessories are like badges – they can tell people something about the kind of person we are. They can reveal our beliefs, our ideas, our attitudes or our position in the world. Some people even say you can tell a great deal about a person's **character** just by looking at their shoes. Are the shoes stylish and clean or are they old and scuffed, for example? Are they in a quiet, **conventional** colour, or are they bright and gaudy, drawing lots of attention to the wearer?

Accessories change with fashion and there is nothing that looks more old-fashioned than a bag or a pair of shoes in an out-of-date style. The need to wear shoes continues, but we soon get bored with one style and are eager to try another. Sometimes the variety of styles available is quite bewildering.

Teenagers often like to express their personality by wearing anything that their parents would dislike. For example, the way a punk dresses can signal two things: that he or she belongs to a group of people who share similar ideas about fashion and dress; and that he or she rejects the way adults would like them to dress.

Today, young people have a great variety of fashionable 'looks' to follow because fashions are constantly changing.

Above Accessories can complement the look you are trying to create. Maria's hair, make-up and earrings give an overall dramatic effect. Tony has gone for a more subtle fashionable look with a simple earring and brooch.

Newspapers can be an important accessory for business people, because the particular newspaper you read can often give other people an idea of the kind of person you are.

Business people hope to show their reliability and **professionalism** by carrying a smart briefcase and wearing shoes that are carefully polished.

Look at me!

One of the easiest ways to gain attention is to wear something outrageous. Some people are famous for their **extravagant** use of accessories. For example, everyone who has seen Dame Edna Everage (the Australian comic character played by Barry Humphries) remembers the many different pairs of bizarre glasses she wears. They draw attention to Dame Edna's face and make the audience laugh even before she has started to speak.

In the competitive world of pop music, many groups and pop personalities find that certain ways of dressing can prove a useful and memorable **gimmick**. In the 1970s Elton John wore strange glasses and absolutely outrageous shoes which helped him and his music become noticed. Today, members of the hip-hop pop group Run DMC wear lots of chunky gold jewellery – a gimmick which is copied by their fans.

Dame Edna Everage is a well-known comic character, famous for, amongst other things, her bizarre accessories. She always wears a pair of outrageous and funny glasses, and some false costume jewellery. In this photograph, taken during her performance at the Strand Theatre, London, Dame Edna is also wearing a bright pink wig which adds to the overall comic effect.

Another person famous for her style of accessories is Gertrude Shilling who, each year, turned up at Ascot wearing an even more startling and extravagant hat designed by her son, David. No doubt it provided good publicity for his designs, as a photograph of her could be guaranteed to appear in the national newspapers the following day.

Clowns, and jokers generally, often wear accessories to make us notice them. It may be a revolving bow tie or a buttonhole flower that squirts water at you. Charlie Chaplin will always be associated with his two famous 'props' – his little hat and cane.

Gertrude Shilling wearing a hat designed by her son David.

Below **Boy George and friends wearing some outrageous make-up and accessories that will gain them a lot of attention.**

What accessories can do

Accessories can completely change the appearance of our clothes. This makes them extremely useful, because they can be used to dress up a few simple outfits to give the impression we have a vast wardrobe of different clothes.

A simple, brightly-coloured scarf tied around your head can not only emphasize the colour of your hair but also make you look quite individual.

With the addition of a few colourful badges or pieces of jewellery, dull clothes can be made to look unusual and **individual**. Girls can make themselves look more interesting by putting ribbons or colourful clips in their hair.

Today, watches come in many different colours and styles, from elegant dress watches to bright fashion watches which come in a wide variety of loud, bold and cheerful colours.

Accessories can help us to express our personalities by changing our appearance.

The black shoes, bag and hair accessory worn by this model are a stark and effective contrast to her white suit and tights. The whole look is smart and co-ordinated.

One of the best things about them is that they do not have to be expensive. In fact, you can make some accessories from old bits of metal or clothes. For example, try cutting up some old fabric – a dress, a T-shirt or even an old pair of curtains – and make a belt, scarf or headband out of the material. There are plenty of shops where it is possible to buy big, wooden beads and string them together to make a necklace. You could also gather a collection of cheap jewellery – the kind you can easily find in jumble sales and second-hand shops. Remove the beads and baubles and restring them into necklaces and bracelets of your own design. You could also collect old hats and decorate them with scarves, ribbons, flowers or whatever you wish.

Penny (left) is wearing a small skull cap to complement her short, spiky hair. Faye (right) has brightened up her straw hat by tying a colourful scarf around it.

Above Jo (left) and Lesley have made their casual outfits look chic by wearing smart black hats and stylish earrings.

Right Singer Annie Lennox has a very individual 'look'. Her clever use of accessories – black leather gloves, studs on her clothes and a studded belt – presents an aggressive and interesting image.

At one time fashion books always recommended people to choose a set of matching accessories – gloves, bag, shoes, scarf etc – to give a total look. Nowadays, fashions are much freer, especially amongst young people. You can experiment, be adventurous and express your own personality.

13

Chapter 3

Useful Accessories

Footwear

There are many different styles of footwear worn around the world. In fact, there is a type of shoe or boot for almost every kind of climate or lifestyle.

One of the most popular kinds of shoe in the world today is the training shoe. Originally, this was designed for sports wear, but now it is increasingly worn as an

There is a wide variety of training shoes available. Most people wear training shoes as comfortable, everyday footwear. They are also very popular amongst joggers and other sports people because they are light and flexible. This jogger is running in Sun Valley in Idaho, USA.

everyday shoe. The training shoe is so popular because it is light, moulded to the foot for comfort, soft and easy to wear. The uppers may be plastic or leather, but the soles are usually made from hard-wearing, man-made materials.

In various parts of the world specialized footwear developed to suit the particular climate and available natural resources. The **Inuit** of the Arctic used animal furs to make boots that kept them warm in cold, icy conditions. Native Americans used animal hides, stitched together with leather, to make soft **moccasins**. To cope with hot conditions, sandals were developed to allow the maximum air to circulate around the foot. Today, there is a great variety of sandals available.

The Inuit people, who live in very cold conditions in arctic North America and Greenland, need a special type of clothing and footwear to cope with the freezing conditions.

Black leather gloves are an extremely stylish fashion accessory.

Gloves and scarves

There are hundreds of different styles of gloves to protect our hands and also to keep them warm. Some gloves are made of soft leather or fine silk and are worn by rich or fashionable people. Some are made of rubber or plastic and are worn as protection by people such as surgeons doing operations, or laboratory workers who have to handle dangerous chemicals. Others are specially designed for use in a particular sport, such as a baseball mitt or a cricket glove. American football players wear special padded gloves. These protect the players' hands from injuries.

Most gloves are based on the shape of the hand, allowing the fingers to move even when the gloves are worn. **Mittens**, however, keep hands warm by putting all the fingers together in one bag-shaped glove. **Muffs** keep both hands warm in a fur bag worn on a string around the neck. In the past, fingerless gloves were popular with street traders as they kept their hands warm and, at the same time, their fingers were free to pick up goods and money. Today, they have become popular fashion items with young people.

Scarves are meant to protect our heads and throats, but often they are worn mainly as decoration. Many scarves are printed with interesting designs and patterns and are worn around the head and tied to complement an outfit. College scarves are often worn as a sort of badge, identifying the particular college the wearer belongs to.

Above Luke Goss, from the popular pop group Bros, is wearing a colourful scarf tied casually around his neck as a fashion accessory.

Left Scarves come in many colours, materials and designs. Many people wear scarves as part of an outfit – a dress and head-dress in matching material, for example.

Hats

Different styles of hats have developed in various parts of the world, influenced mainly by climate and available materials. Most people need some kind of head protection in both hot and cold weather. Hats can protect our eyes from the glare of the sun and prevent us from getting **sunstroke**. In cold weather, hats can keep our ears warm and stop our body heat from escaping.

The wide-brimmed **sombrero** comes, originally, from Mexico where it was useful in giving shade from the hot sun. The freezing cold Russian winter encouraged people to wear hats made of fur, knitted **balaclava helmets**, and warm, fur-lined hoods for protection.

Above Remember when choosing a hat to make sure it suits the shape of your face and your particular hair-style. Lizzie, for example, wears a large hat with a wide brim to balance her long, thick hair.

Left Hats have an important practical function for many people. This police officer in Sydney, Australia wears a hat as part of her uniform. She is giving the little boy a safety helmet in case he falls off his bicycle and hurts his head.

Above Racing drivers travel at extremely fast speeds around tracks. They need tough helmets to protect their heads in case of an accident.

Imagine how difficult it must be to wear a hat like this! It has been hand-knitted, using real wool, into the shape of the Leaning Tower of Pisa.

Hats can also be an important fashion accessory. Today, they are worn mainly at weddings or important functions. However, baseball caps and fashion hats are becoming more and more popular as everyday wear.

Many hats are worn as part of a uniform, such as those worn by nurses, chauffeurs, ticket collectors and police officers. Other hats and helmets protect people at work, such as fire officers, building site workers, miners and racing drivers.

Bags and belts

We all have to carry things around with us, whether it be school books, shopping or papers for work. How many different types of bags can you think of? There are so many kinds, from the simple plastic carrier bag to the chic, expensive leather handbag, that it is possible to find a style that suits you.

It is odd that in many countries it is still not acceptable for men to carry bags. Women can carry huge handbags bulging with papers, purses and belongings. Men, however, seem to prefer to carry their

These Japanese children carry their books to school in practical, yellow satchels.

loose change and other belongings around in trouser or jacket pockets or **anonymous**-looking briefcases.

There are bags for special occasions, such as the sports bag. You can also buy bags specially for use on the beach, delicate bags for wearing with evening dresses, or **rucksacks** that strap on your back leaving your hands free for climbing or cycling.

Belts are very important accessories, whether they are holding up a skirt or a pair of trousers, or whether they are simply decorating an outfit. Changing the belt on a dress, or adding one to a long shirt, can completely alter the style and look you are creating.

Above **Rucksacks are very useful for people who are on walking or climbing holidays. They are worn on the back which leaves the hands free.**

Belts are a useful accessory because not only do they decorate an outfit but they can give extra shape to the wearer's body.

Umbrellas

The first umbrellas were very simple affairs – just a large plant leaf on a stalk held above the head as protection from heat and rain. This original basic design was developed into our modern umbrellas and **parasols**.

Japanese and Chinese parasols are beautifully made from pleated paper, decorated with painted designs. Like umbrellas, they can be folded down for easy carrying.

Umbrellas are much stronger. They are mostly made of a metal framework of spokes covered in nylon fabric to keep off the rain. Some are long and are carried rather like a walking stick. Others can be folded away to fit into a bag or briefcase. In big cities on a wet day you can see a huge

Above **Decorating beautiful paper parasols in the village of Chang Mai in Thailand.**

Below **The crowd at a Wimbledon tennis match which was washed out.**

variety of different coloured umbrellas being carried along.

In recent years several new designs have been tried out. For example, it was fashionable a few years ago to carry mushroom-shaped, **transparent** umbrellas that came down over your shoulders and enabled you to see where you were going. Many umbrellas now have carrying straps built into them so they can be carried over the shoulder. You can also get huge, special umbrellas, mostly used by golfers, made of large, brightly coloured panels.

Notice the variety of colours and types of umbrellas in the above photograph.

Chapter 4

Decorative Accessories

Precious jewels

Jewellery, to most of us, consists of a pretty but cheap pair of earrings or bracelet, badge or brooch. However, there is one particular kind of jewellery that most of us will never afford – rare or precious jewels.

For thousands of years gold and rare **gems** have been worked into beautiful pieces of jewellery to decorate the clothing of important people. Gold and silver have been made into rings, necklaces, **armlets**, **anklets**, brooches and tie pins.

Left to right: Duke of Edinburgh, Queen Sophia of Spain, Queen Elizabeth II and King Juan Carlos of Spain.

Above Some of the rare gems that were part of the Duchess of Windsor's collection.

Below International film star Elizabeth Taylor is famous for her jewellery collection.

Diamonds, rubies, emeralds and, amethysts are all precious stones, valuable because of their beauty and rarity. Some of the most spectacular stones have belonged to various members of royal families from all over the world. We do not think of these as fashion accessories because they are not worn to complement an outfit but to display power and wealth.

One of the most famous modern collections of jewellery was put on sale in 1987. The jewels belonged to the Duchess of Windsor, the American divorcée who married the Duke of Windsor (King Edward VIII) when he abdicated (gave up) the British throne.

Today, new jewels and metals, such as titanium, have been used to make decorative accessories. It is now possible to buy artificial diamonds, although they are still quite expensive.

Jewellery around the world

Human beings always seem to have enjoyed decorating their bodies with jewellery. People who live in hot climates and, therefore, do not need to wear much clothing, make and wear interesting pieces of jewellery. All kinds of things can be used to decorate our bodies, from beaten metal to feathers, shells, seeds and animal bones. In the past it was believed that these objects had magical powers and could bring good luck.

Right **Beautiful necklaces and head-dresses worn by a mother and daughter in Kashmir.**

Colourful, beaded jewellery worn by two Samburu women in Africa.

This girl from Burkina Faso in West Africa wears colourful beads and shells in her hair and ears and around her neck as decoration. Her overall look is interesting and individual.

In ancient times, people often wore bands around their arms called armlets. Similar bands, called anklets, were worn around the legs. Brooches were worn to fasten pieces of clothing together – buttons had not been invented at this stage. In some cultures both men and women wore long earrings, which were regarded as a sign of high standing in society. It has become fashionable again today for men to have either one or both ears pierced.

Chapter

5

Accessories from the Past

The things they wore!

As fashions change some accessories have disappeared into history. Here are a few examples of accessories that are no longer fashionable. They must have either been uncomfortable or difficult to wear.

In **Elizabethan** times in England it was

Elizabeth I, who was Queen of England between 1558 and 1603, wearing a ruff which was an extremely fashionable accessory in those days. Ruffs were stiff and uncomfortable – fashionable clothes and accessories are not always very practical.

These bizarre clothes were at the height of fashion in Europe in the fifteenth century. The hats and shoes may look ridiculous to us now, but do you think people will laugh at our accessories in 500 years time?

fashionable for men and women to wear ruffs – stiff frills that surround the neck. At the height of their popularity they were completely circular and measured about 400mm in diameter. They had to be held up with a stiff wire frame. The fabric they were made from was stiffened with starch and must have made head movement very difficult indeed.

In the eighteenth century in Europe, bizarre and extraordinary wigs were extremely fashionable amongst the rich. False hair and cotton wool padding were added to the wigs to give extra height. The wigs would also be smeared with hair ointment and powdered. Then they would be decorated with flowers and ribbons. Anxious to outdo each other, some people even went to the extraordinary lengths of adding model coaches and horses, and sometimes even model soldiers in battle on to the wigs!

Shoe fashions have been equally bizarre. In China foot-binding shoes were worn by young girls to stop their feet from growing so they would be kept fashionably small. Much more recently, in the early 1970s, **platform shoes** were extremely fashionable, yet now they look most unattractive and uncomfortable.

Glossary

Anklets Bands worn around the ankle for decoration.
Anonymous Something which has no name or character.
Armlets Bands worn around the arm for decoration.
Balaclava helmets Woollen hats that cover the whole head and neck, leaving only the face uncovered.
Character The special things about someone or something that makes them different from everything and everyone else.
Conventional Following rules or traditions that everyone accepts.
Elizabethan Refers to the period of English history when Elizabeth I was queen (1558–1603).
Extravagant Very loud and showy.
Gems Precious stones.
Gimmick An unusual action or object that is used to gain attention.
Individual Something which is to do with one person or one thing only.
Inuit People from arctic North America and Greenland.
Mittens Bag-shaped gloves that do not have separate sections for fingers.
Moccasins Soft leather shoes originally worn by Native Americans.
Muffs Bags, often made of fur, worn round the neck on a string and used to put the hands in to keep them warm.
Parasols Types of umbrellas used for protection against the sun.
Platform shoes Shoes that are built on high soles and have high heels.
Pliable Flexible or easily bent.
Professionalism Serious and proper attitude towards something like a career.
Rucksacks Bags with straps worn on the back so that the hands are left free for other activities.
Sombrero A broad-rimmed hat worn in Spain and Mexico, amongst other places, as protection against the sun.
Sunstroke A sickness caused by being in the sun for too long. The symptoms are weakness and a high temperature.
Transparent Something which is so light that you can see through it.

Books to read

Childrens's Clothes by Miriam Moss (Wayland, 1988)
Clothes in History by Charlotte Sewell (Wayland, 1983)
Costumes and Clothes by Jean Cooke (Wayland, 1986)
Fashionable Clothes by Miriam Moss (Wayland, 1988)
Fashion and Clothes by Jack Harvey (Macdonald Educational, 1983)
Just Look at Clothes by Brenda Ralph Lewis (Macdonald Educational, 1986)
Twentieth Century Fashion by Eleanor van Zandt (Wayland, 1988)

Index

Accessories
  decorative 4, 5, 24–7
  fashion 6–13, 19
  from the past 28–9
  fun 9
  individual 10
  making 12
  matching 13
  outrageous 8
  teenage 6, 7
  useful 4, 5, 14–23
Amethysts 25
Anklets 24, 27
Armlets 24, 27
Australia 18

Badges 24
Bags 4, 5, 6, 11, 13, 20–21, 22
Balaclava helmets 18
Baseball caps 19
Basic clothing 4
Belts 4, 12, 21
Boots 4, 14, 15
Bows 5
Bow ties 9
Bracelets 12, 24
Briefcases 7, 21, 22
Brooches 7, 24, 27
Bros 17
Business people 7
Buttons 5, 27

Chaplin, Charlie 9
Clips 10
Clowns 9
Coats 4

Diamonds 25

Earrings 7, 13, 27
Edinburgh, Duke of 24
Emeralds 25
Everage, Dame Edna 8

Feathers 26
Flowers 12, 29
Footwear 14–15

Gems 24
George, Boy 9
Glasses, 4, 8
Gloves 5, 13, 16, 17
  fingerless 17
Gold 24
Goss, Luke 17

Hats 4, 5, 12, 13, 18–19
  outrageous 9
Helmets 19

Inuit 15

Jewellery 4, 8, 10, 12
  precious 24–5
John, Elton 8
Joggers 14
Jumpers 4

King Juan Carlos of Spain 24

Lennox, Annie 13

Make-up 9
Mittens 17
Moccasins 15
Muffs 17

Native Americans 15
Newspapers 7

Parasols 22
Police officers 18
Pop music 8
Props 9
Punk clothes 6

Queen
  Elizabeth I 28
  Elizabeth II 24
  Sophia of Spain 24

Racing drivers 19
Ribbons 5, 10, 12, 29
Rings 24

Royal families 24, 25
Rubies 25
Rucksacks 21
Ruffs 28
Run DMC 8

Sandals 15
Satchels 20
Scarves 12, 13, 17
  college 17
  for the head 10
School children 20
Seeds 26
Shells 26
Shilling, Gertrude 9
Shoes 4, 5, 6, 7, 11, 13, 14, 29
  training 14–15
Silver 24
Skirts 4, 21
Sombrero 18
Studs 13
Sun-glasses 5

Taylor, Elizabeth 25
Thailand 22
Tie pins 24
Tights 11
Titanium 25
Trousers 4, 21

Umbrellas 4, 22–3
Uniforms 19
USA 14

Watches 10
Wigs 8, 29
Wimbledon 22
Windsor, Duke and Duchess
  of 25

Picture acknowledgements

The Publisher would like to thank the following for supplying the pictures used in this book: All-Action Photographic 6, 9 (bottom), 13 (bottom), 17 (top right); David Bowden 18 (bottom left); Camera Press 11; Bruce Coleman Limited 22 (top); Mary Evans Picture Library 29; Hutchison Library 9 (top), 26 (top); Paul Seheult 4 (top right), 5 (bottom), 7 (top), 10, 12, 13 (top), 18 (top right), 21 (bottom left); Topham Picture Library COVER, 8, 16, 19 (bottom), 22 (bottom), 23, 24, 25, 27; Wayland Picture Library 28; ZEFA 4 (bottom left), 5 (top), 7 (bottom left), 19 (top), 20, 21 (top right), 26 (bottom).